ABSOLUTE BEGINNERS

Guitar Chords

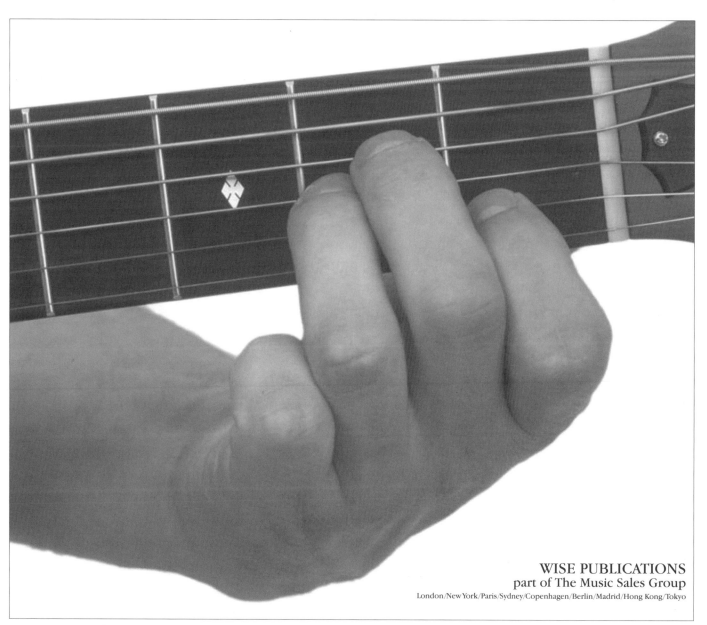

WISE PUBLICATIONS
part of The Music Sales Group
London/New York/Paris/Sydney/Copenhagen/Berlin/Madrid/Hong Kong/Tokyo

GW00776061

Published by
Wise Publications
14-15 Berners Street, London, W1T 3LJ

Exclusive Distributors:
Music Sales Limited
Distribution Centre,
Newmarket Road, Bury St Edmunds,
Suffolk, IP33 3YB, UK.

Music Sales Corporation
180 Madison Avenue, 24th Floor,
New York NY 10016, USA.

Music Sales Pty Limited
4th floor, Lisgar House,
30-32 Carrington Street, Sydney,
NSW 2000, Australia.

Order No. AM969661R
ISBN 978-1-78558-468-8
This book © Copyright 2002 by Wise Publications,
a division of Music Sales Limited.

Unauthorised reproduction of any part of this publication by any
means including photocopying is an infringement of copyright.

Compiled and written by Sorcha Armstrong.
Photographs by George Taylor.
Book design by Chloë Alexander.
Models: Arthur Dick and Andrew King.
Audio recorded by Joe Bennett.
Guitars by Joe Bennett.

Printed in the EU.

Your Guarantee of Quality:
As publishers, we strive to produce every book to the highest
commercial standards. This book has been carefully designed
to minimise awkward page turns and to make playing from it a
real pleasure. Particular care has been given to specifying acid-
free, neutral-sized paper made from pulps which have not been
elemental chlorine bleached. This pulp is from farmed sustainable
forests and was produced with special regard for the environment.
Throughout, the printing and binding have been planned to
ensure a sturdy, attractive publication which should give years of
enjoyment. If your copy fails to meet our high standards, please
inform us and we will gladly replace it.

Got any comments?
e-mail **absolutebeginners@musicsales.co.uk**

www.musicsales.com

Contents

Introduction

Welcome to *Absolute Beginners Guitar Chords*! This book will show you all the chords you need to know to play thousands of songs, and increase your knowledge of the guitar.

If you've got *Absolute Beginners Guitar*, you'll already know 10 of the most basic and useful chords. *Absolute Beginners Guitar Book Two* took you through another 12. These are all shown on pages 8-11 as a handy reference.

In this book, you'll learn more of the chords guitarists use most often. All the major chord types are here, including major, minor, 7s, suspended chords, barre and moveable chords, power-chords and many others!

All you need to get started is to load up the audio, tune up and follow the easy diagrams and photos.

Tuning Notes **Track 1**

How To Read Fretboxes

Each new chord has been arranged using the same easy-to-read format you used in Absolute Beginners Guitar. Here's how to decipher the information:

Fretbox
Fretboxes show the guitar next upright, i.e. with the headstock, nut and tuning pegs at the top of the picture – six vertical lines represent the strings. From left to right, they are E, A, D, G, B, E.

Chord photo
These are shown 'over the shoulder' – as you would see it.

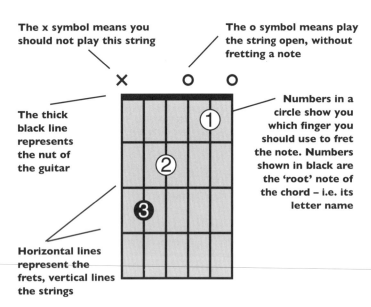

The x symbol means you should not play this string

The o symbol means play the string open, without fretting a note

The thick black line represents the nut of the guitar

Numbers in a circle show you which finger you should use to fret the note. Numbers shown in black are the 'root' note of the chord – i.e. its letter name

Horizontal lines represent the frets, vertical lines the strings

Tablature
'TAB' is drawn with the guitar on its side, with the thickest string at the bottom – six horizontal lines represent the strings. If you've got *Absolute Beginners Guitar Book Two*, you'll already be familiar with TAB.

In this example, the top stave shows the chord as it would appear in traditional music notation. The TAB is below and shows fret positions using numbers. There is no indication of which fingers to use. A zero means that the string should be played open.

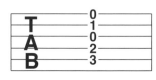

If a finger is laid flat to hold down two or more strings, this is called a 'barre' and symbolised by a curved line over the strings being held down.

In this book, we'll be talking about 'barre' or 'moveable' chords – so called because one of the fretting hand's fingers is pressed against two or more strings (this is shown as a curved line in the fretbox).

They can be moved up or down the neck to different fret positions to create new chords. The advantage of this is that once you've learned one new barre shape, you've in effect learned 12 new chords!

Below are diagrams showing the names of the notes on the sixth and fifth strings.

To find any barre chord, look at the fretbox to see whether the root note (shown in a black circle) appears on the fifth or sixth string, then move the barre shape up or down until you reach the desired pitch. For example, a chord of A♭ (also known as G♯) can be played using an 'F shape', moved up to the 4th fret.

You'll find these diagrams useful when you get to the section on barre chords (page 32). You'll be able to figure out many more chords using these diagrams, and the chord shapes shown.

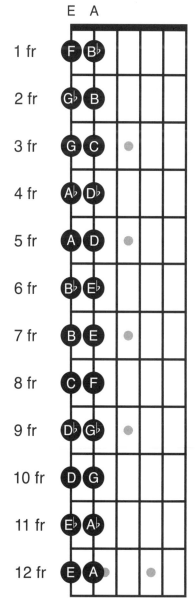

This diagram shows how to find any barre chord position, and will help you if the chord you want has a sharp (♯) in its name. All of the F-based barre shapes in this book (see page 32) have their root on the sixth string – the B♭ based ones have their root on the fifth.

Use this version if the chord you want has a flat (♭) in its name. Both of these diagrams can be used to find any barre chord which has its root on the sixth or fifth string – simply select the type you want (minor, maj7, 7 etc) then find the letter name (F, G, D♭ etc) on the fingerboard.

Chord Summary

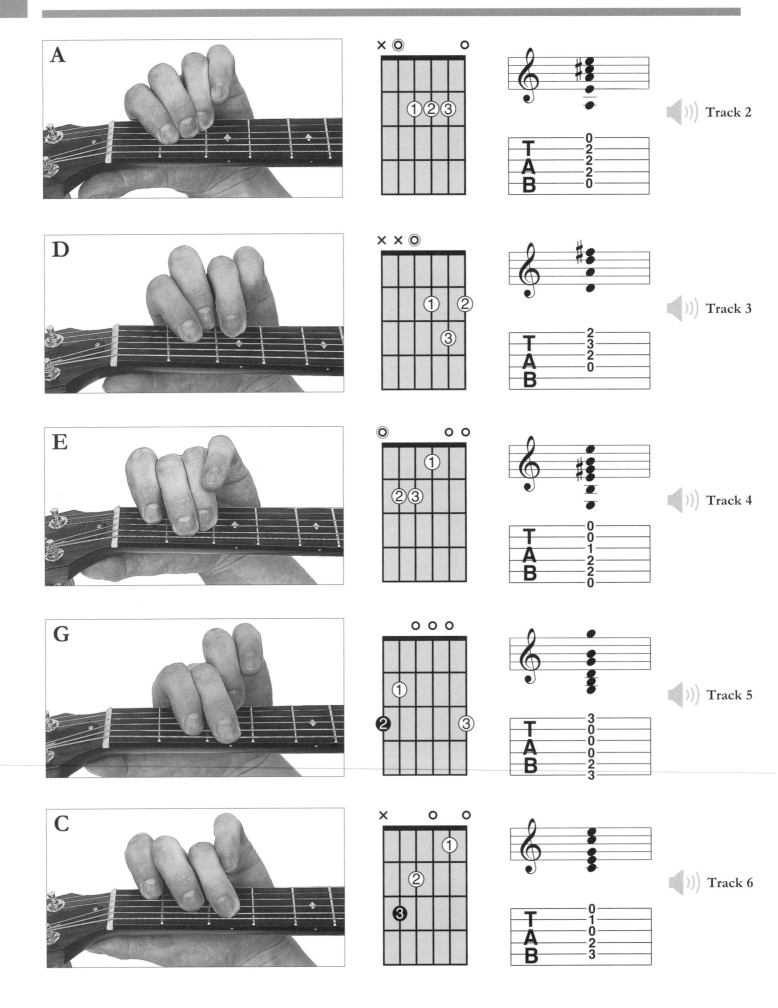

A — Track 2

D — Track 3

E — Track 4

G — Track 5

C — Track 6

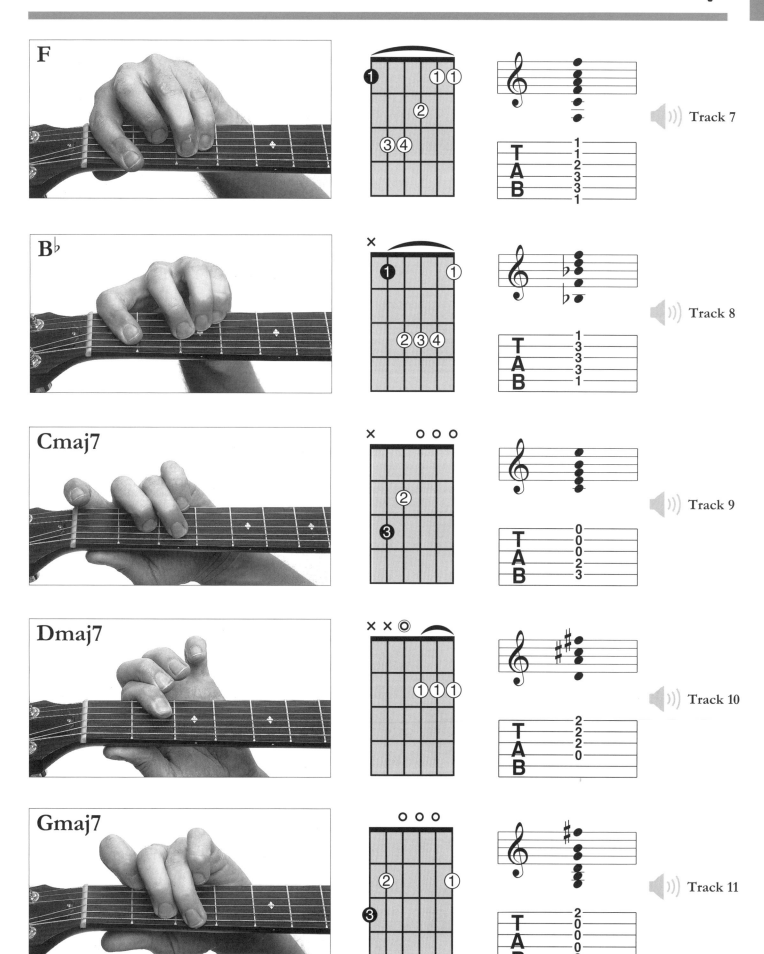

F

Track 7

B♭

Track 8

Cmaj7

Track 9

Dmaj7

Track 10

Gmaj7

Track 11

Chord Summary

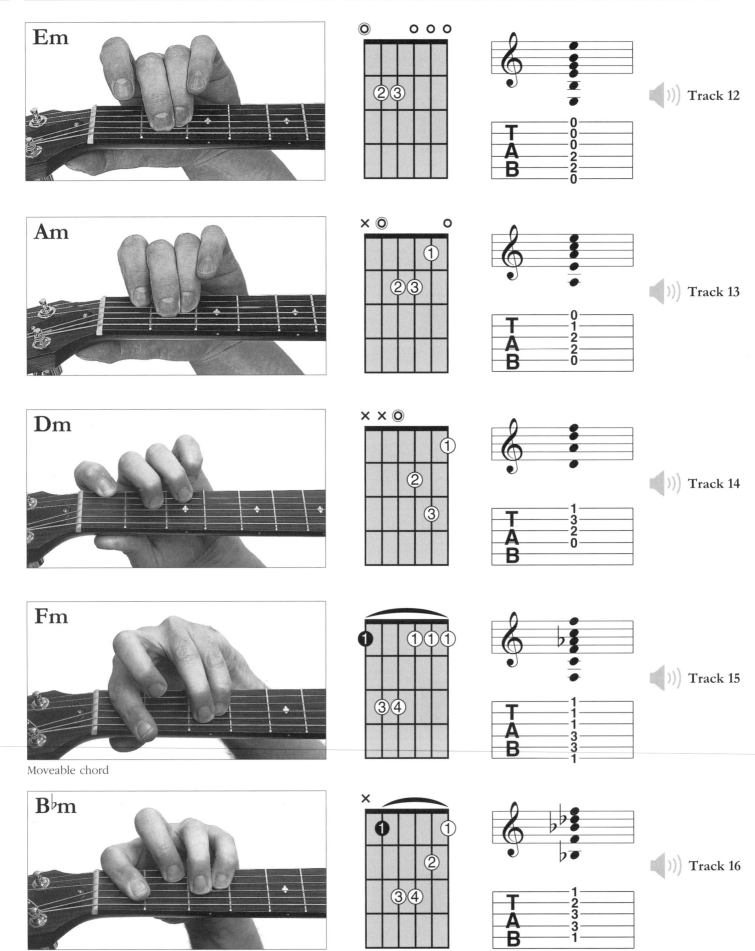

Em

Track 12

Am

Track 13

Dm

Track 14

Fm

Moveable chord

Track 15

B♭m

Moveable chord

Track 16

D7

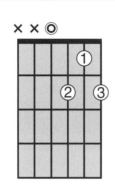
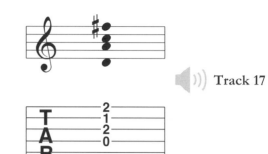

Track 17

E7

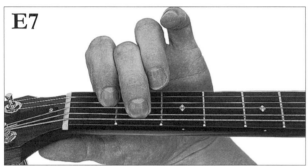
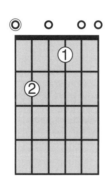
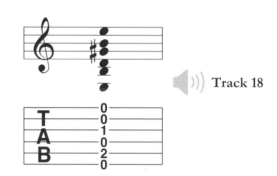

Track 18

A7

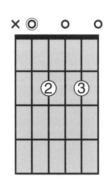
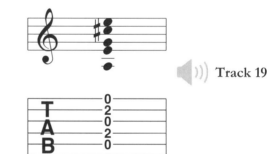

Track 19

B7

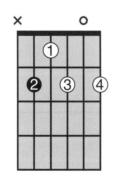
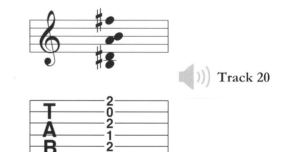

Track 20

Em7

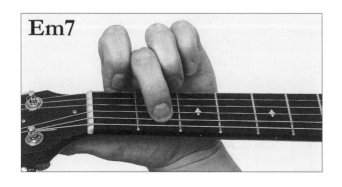
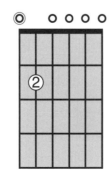
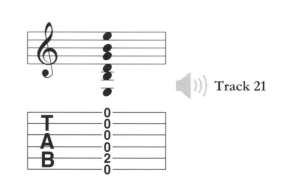

Track 21

C7

Adding your litte finger to a normal C major shape gives this easy open version of C7. Remember not to hit the bottom E string.

 **Track 22**

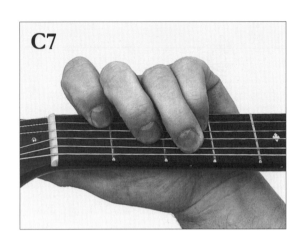

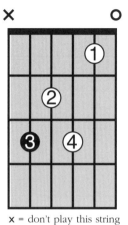

x = don't play this string
o = open string

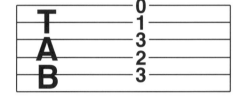

```
T    0
A    1
     3
     2
B    3
```

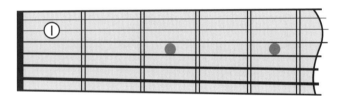

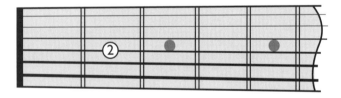

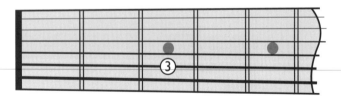
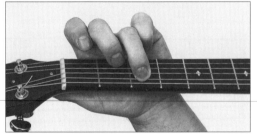

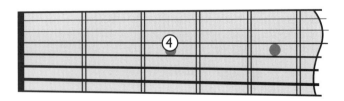

This open G7 shape looks very similar to an ordinary G major chord, but the fingering is totally different.

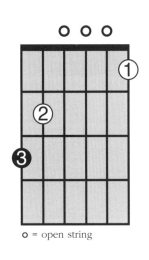

o = open string

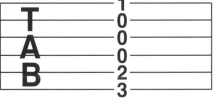

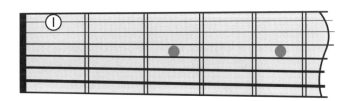

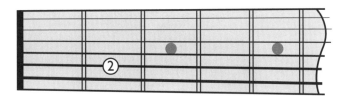

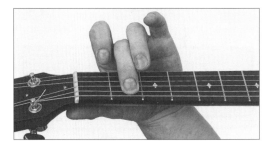

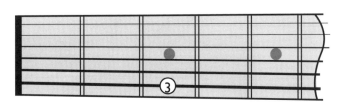

Final chord shape

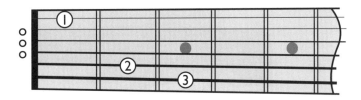

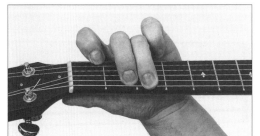

o = open string

A major 7

The fingering for this chord looks a lot like the open D7 chord shape. Try moving this shape around the fretboard for some interesting chord sounds!

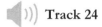 **Track 24**

Amaj7

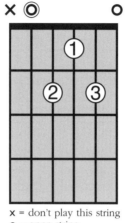

x = don't play this string
o = open string

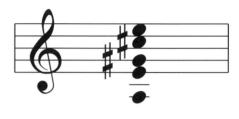

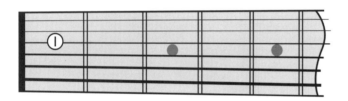

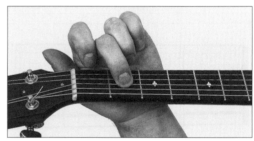

Final chord shape

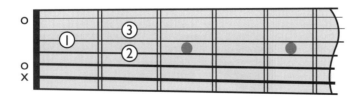

X = don't play this string   **O** = open string

This is a rarer chord, used mostly in country-style strumming or single-note picked parts.

 Track 25

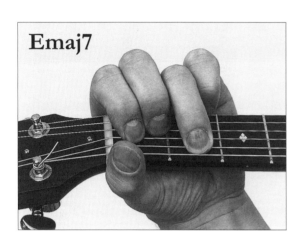

Emaj7

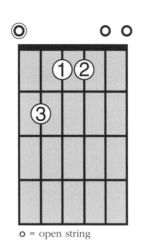

o = open string

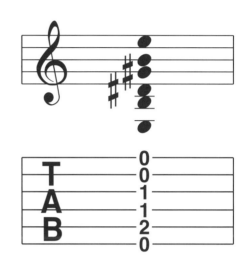

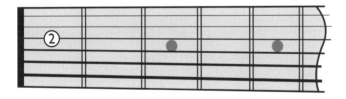

Final chord shape

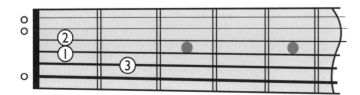

o = open string

F major 7

This nice simple chord shape sounds great with a C or C major 7 chord before or after it.

Track 26

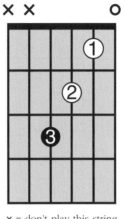

x = don't play this string
o = open string

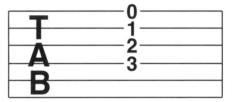

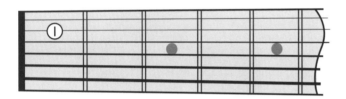

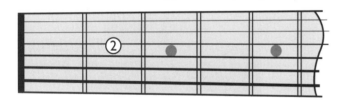

Final chord shape

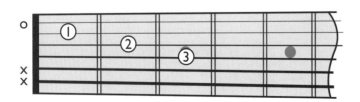

X = don't play this string   O = open string

Take your third finger off the open A minor chord, and you get Am7. Remember not to play the sixth string!

Track 27

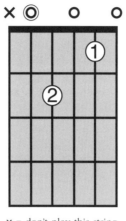

x = don't play this string
o = open string

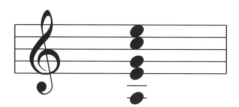

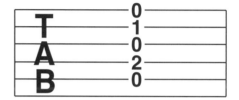

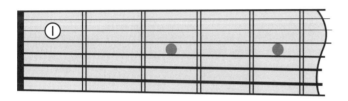

Final chord shape

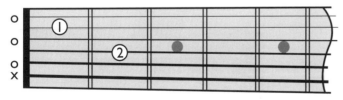

X = don't play this string   O = open string

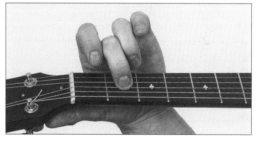

D minor 7

You can play this chord in two different ways – using a partial barre as shown here, or using three separate fingers for the three fretted notes.

 **Track 28**

Dm7

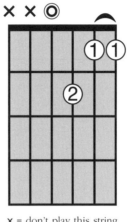

x = don't play this string
o = open string

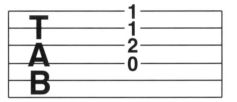

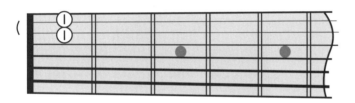

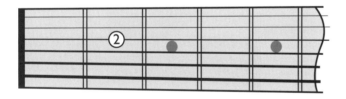

Final chord shape

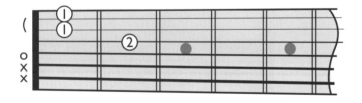

X = don't play this string   O = open string

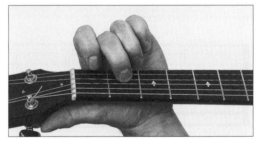

Hold down a standard A major shape, then use the fourth finger to add the extra note on the third fret. Playing Asus4 followed by A creates a nice effect.

 **Track 29**

Asus4

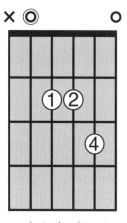

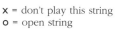

x = don't play this string
o = open string

```
    0
T   3
    2
A   2
B   0
```

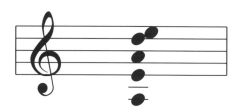

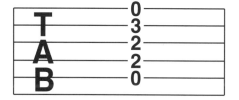

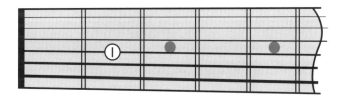

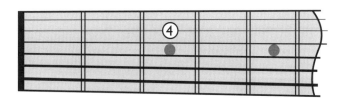

Final chord shape

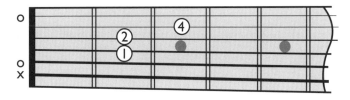

X = don't play this string   **O** = open string

D sus 4

Like Asus4, you can keep the standard D shape, and just add your fourth finger at the third fret to make it easier to change back to D.

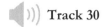 Track 30

Dsus4

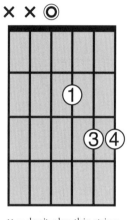

x = don't play this string
o = open string

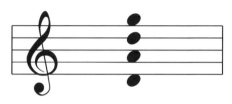

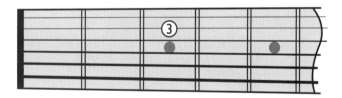

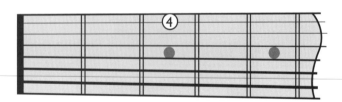

Final chord shape

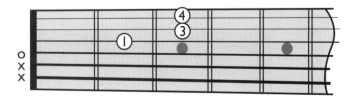

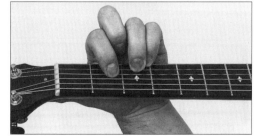

X = don't play this string   O = open string

This chord can be played with either the fingering shown here (which makes it easier to change to an E chord) or the fingering for an A chord shape.

 **Track 31**

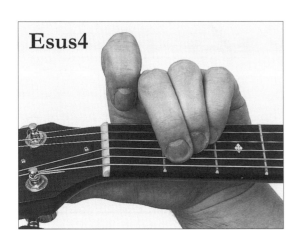

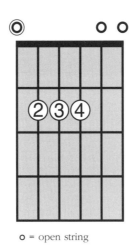

o = open string

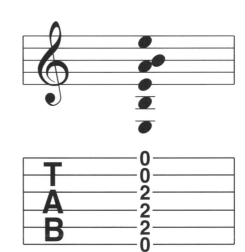

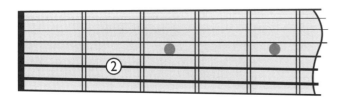

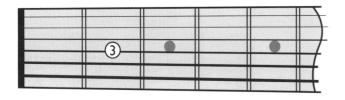

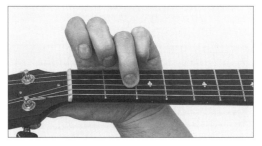

Final chord shape

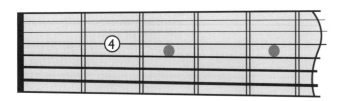

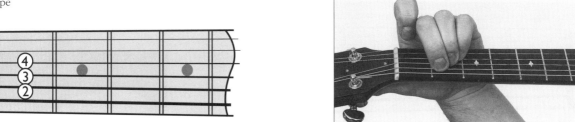

o = open string

G sus 4

This fingering is useful if you're playing a G major chord after it. You can also play the shape with a finger on the 5th string at the 2nd fret.

 Track 32

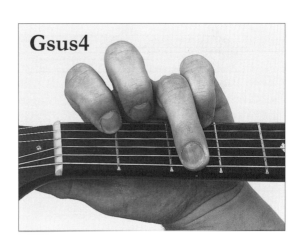

Gsus4

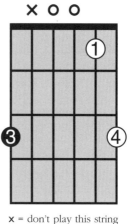

x = don't play this string
o = open string

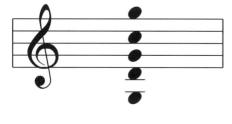

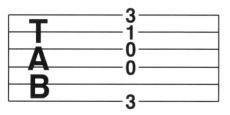

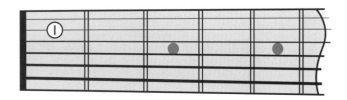

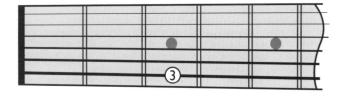

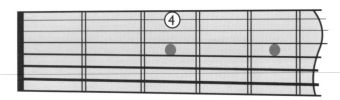

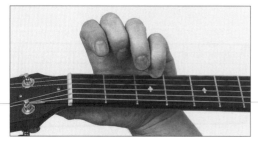

Final chord shape

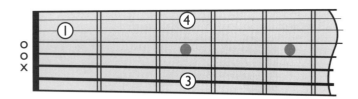

X = don't play this string   O = open string

This moveable barre chord shape can be used
to create a sus4 chord elsewhere on the fretboard.
See page 32 for more on moveable chords.

See page 32 for more on moveable chords.

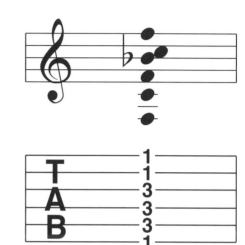

Track 33

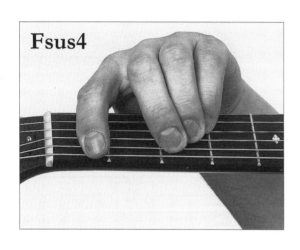

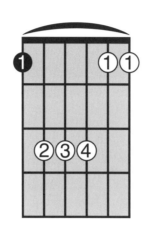

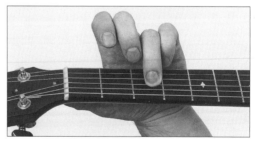

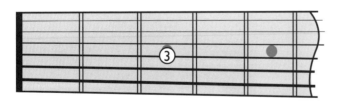

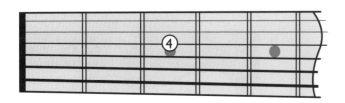

A sus 2

This is one of those great chords that sounds more complicated than it actually is, and is a favourite amongst acoustic guitarists.

 Track 34

Asus2

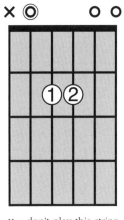

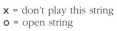

x = don't play this string
o = open string

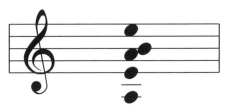

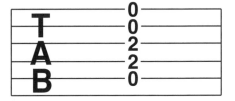

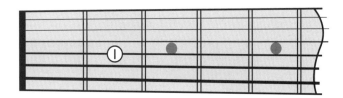

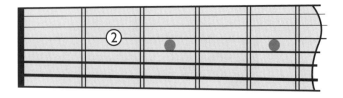

Final chord shape

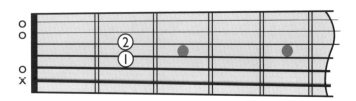

X = don't play this string   O = open string

Just finger a D major chord and take your third finger off to create this open Dsus2 shape.

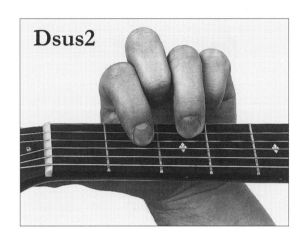

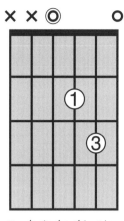

x = don't play this string
o = open string

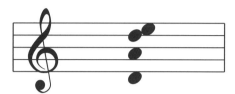

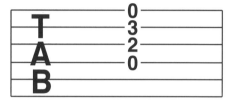

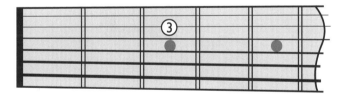

Final chord shape

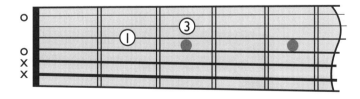

X = don't play this string   O = open string

F5

You can move this shape anywhere on the fretboard to create a power chord. You can also either play all three bass strings, or just the bottom two for a 'heavier' sound.

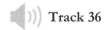

F5

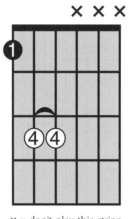

x = don't play this string

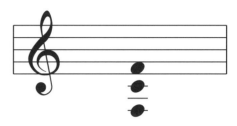

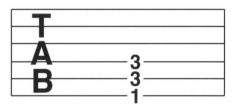

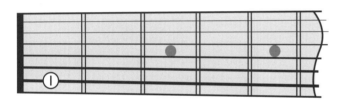

Final chord shape

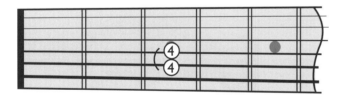

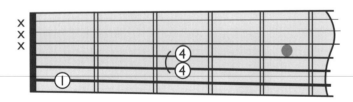

X = don't play this string

There are two ways to play this A5 chord: using the fingering shown below, or the optional 'barre' shape shown at the bottom of the page.

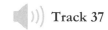 **Track 37**

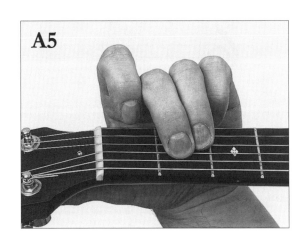

A5

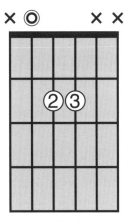

x = don't play this string
o = open string

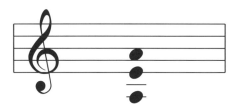

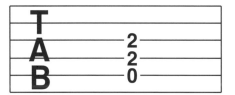

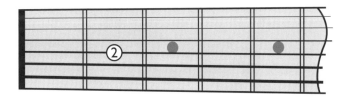

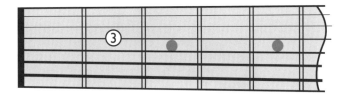

Final chord shape

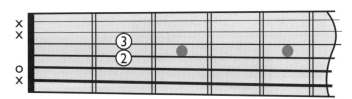

Optional 'barre' fingering

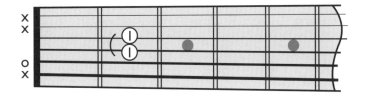

X = don't play this string   O = open string

D5

You can also play a D5 using the A5 shape (page 24) at the 5th fret, with the root note on the 5th string. This is useful if you're moving the same shape around in a sequence.

(page 24)

Track 38

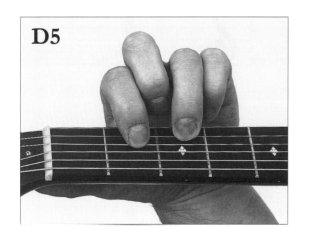

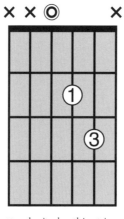

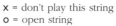

x = don't play this string
o = open string

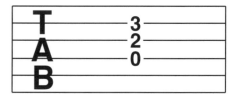

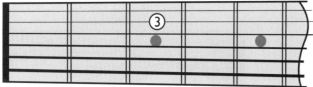

Final chord shape

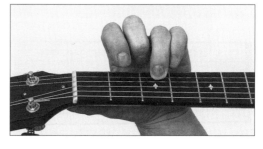

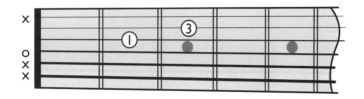

X = don't play this string   **O** = open string

Take your first finger off the fifth string of an alternative G chord and you get this easy G5 shape. Tip: use the side of your second finger to mute the fifth string.

 **Track 39**

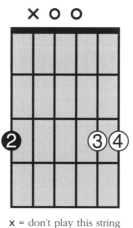

x = don't play this string
o = open string

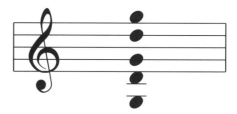

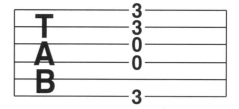

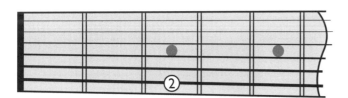

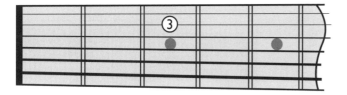

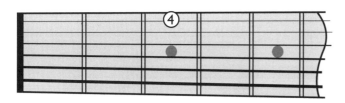

Final chord shape

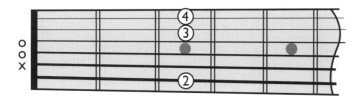

X = don't play this string   O = open string

E5

Play just the bottom three strings of a standard E minor chord, and you get this easy, heavy-sounding power chord shape.

 **Track 40**

E5

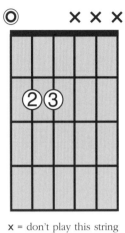

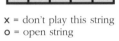

x = don't play this string
o = open string

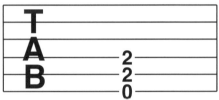

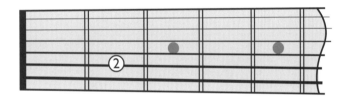

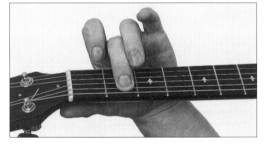

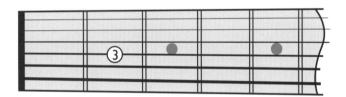

Final chord shape

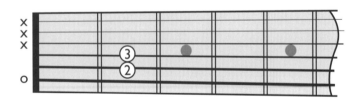

X = don't play this string   O = open string

This chord is a bit of a stretch but worth the practice! To liven up a chord sequence, try using this instead of a normal A major chord.

 **Track 41**

Aadd9

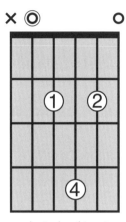

x = don't play this string
o = open string

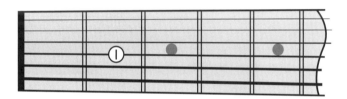

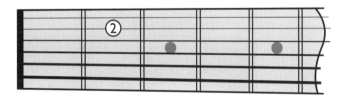

Final chord shape

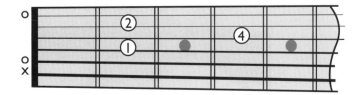

X = don't play this string   **O** = open string

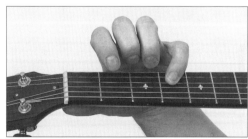

C add 9

This Noel Gallagher favourite is simply an open C major chord with a fourth finger added at the 3rd fret, on the 2nd string.

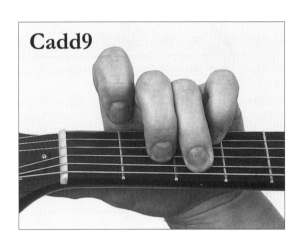

Cadd9

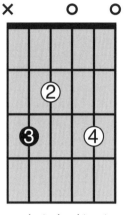

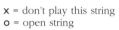

x = don't play this string
o = open string

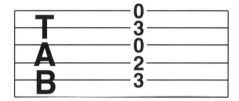

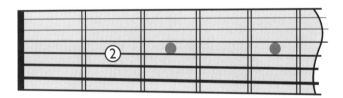

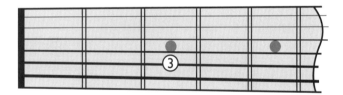

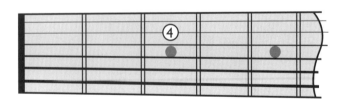

Final chord shape

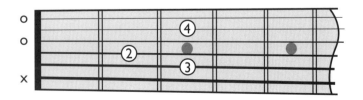

X = don't play this string   O = open string

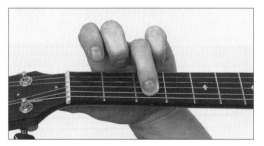

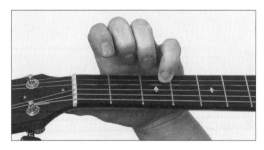

Try picking across the strings of this chord rather than just strumming up and down for an interesting 'heavy metal intro' sound.

 **Track 43**

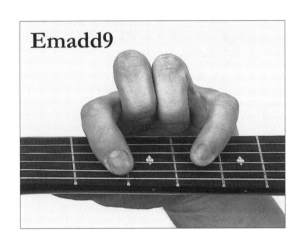

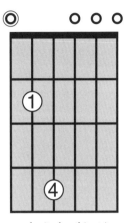

x = don't play this string
o = open string

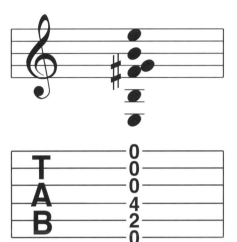

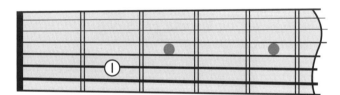

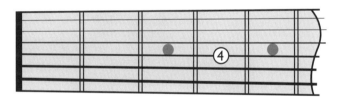

Final chord shape

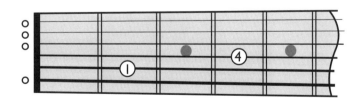

X = don't play this string   O = open string

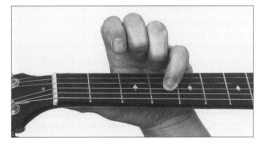

F7 barre

This is quite a tricky chord to hold – you really need to press down hard to get the fourth string to sound. However, it can be moved up the fretboard to make other 7th chords.

Track 44

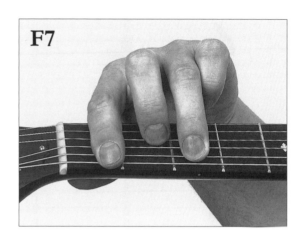

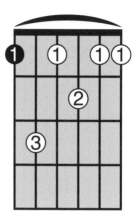

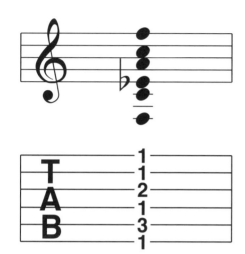

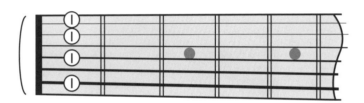

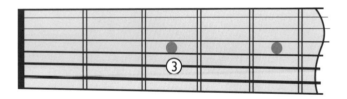

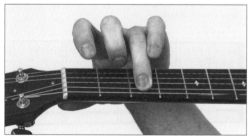

Final chord shape

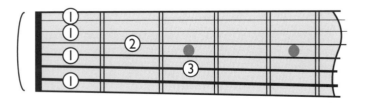

Like F7, this barre chord can be moved up the fretboard to create other Minor 7th chords. You can also try playing a partial version for a funky effect – just strum the top three strings.

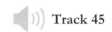 **Track 45**

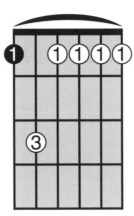

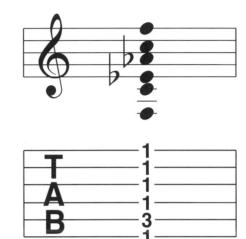

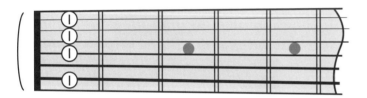

Final chord shape

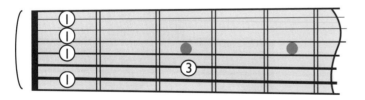

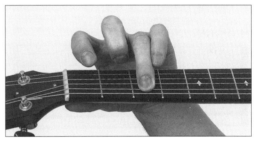

F major 7 barre

Move this chord around on the fretboard to create other Major 7th chords. It's also an idea to avoid playing the top string as it clashes a bit with the note on the fourth string.

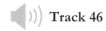 **Track 46**

Fmaj7

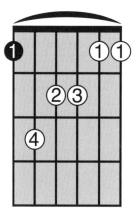

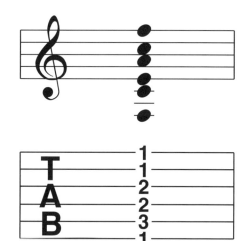

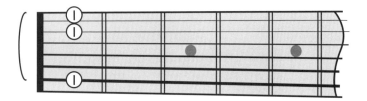

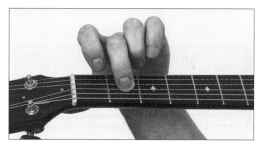

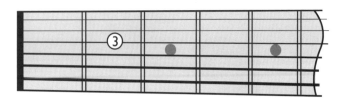

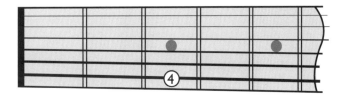

This second moveable 7th chord provides you with another shape which you can use to get more 7th chords up the fretboard. Move this up one fret for B7, two for C7, etc.

 Track 47

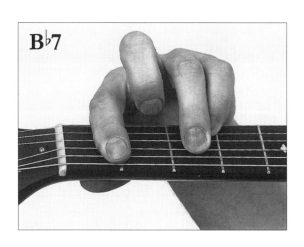

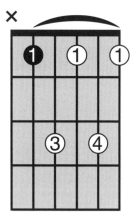

x = don't play this string

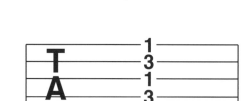

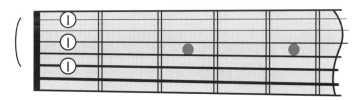

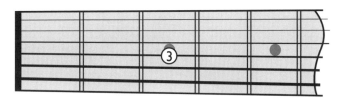

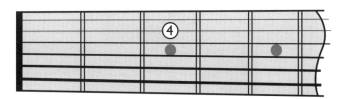

Final chord shape

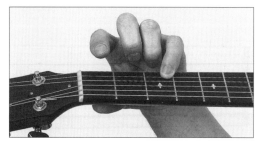

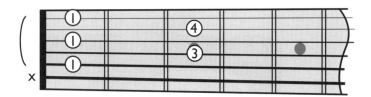

x = don't play this string

B♭m 7 barre

This is a difficult shape but very versatile – it can be used all over the fretboard. Try using it at the 12th fret for a funky sound.

 Track 48

B♭m7

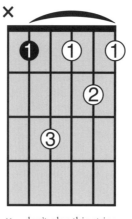

x = don't play this string

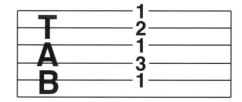

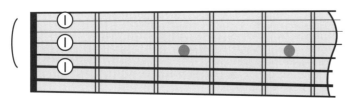

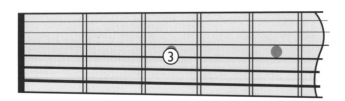

Final chord shape

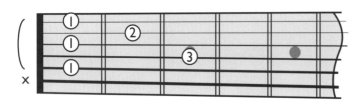

x = don't play this string

This version is more common and better-sounding than the Fmajor7 shape on page 34 – and you don't have to press down a full barre.

 **Track 49**

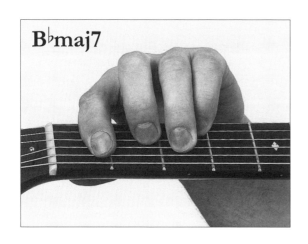

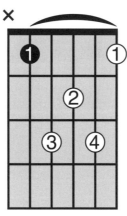

x = don't play this string

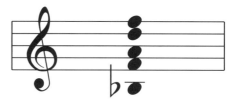

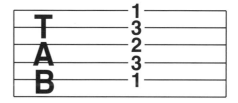

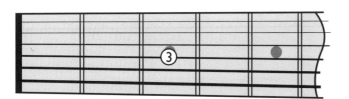

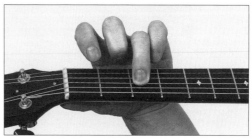

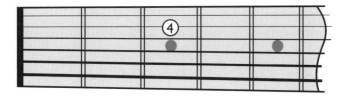

Classic Chords

E9

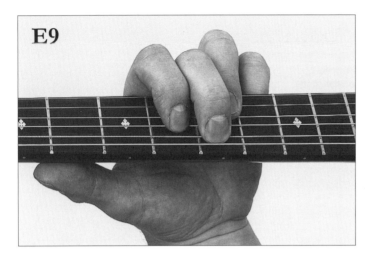

E9

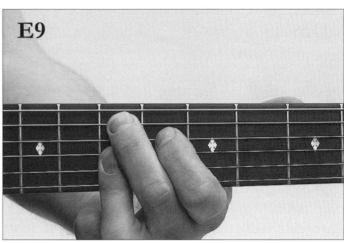

6 fr

Track 50

The James Brown Chord
Play this chord and think 'James Brown'! This classic funky shape has been used in countless James Brown classics and '70s funk and disco tunes. Strum quickly, pressing your fingers on and off the fretboard for that authentic funk sound.

E7#9

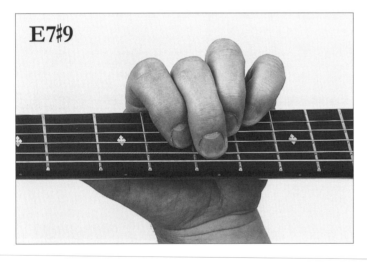

E7#9

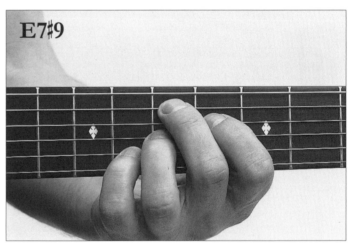

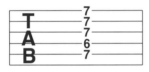

6 fr

Track 51

The Jimi Hendrix Chord
This chord was a Jimi Hendrix favourite – used in songs like 'Purple Haze', 'Foxy Lady' and 'Voodoo Chile'.
It's fairly easy to finger, and as with the previous chord, you'll get a much funkier sound if you play fast, partially muted up and down strums.

Dm11/A

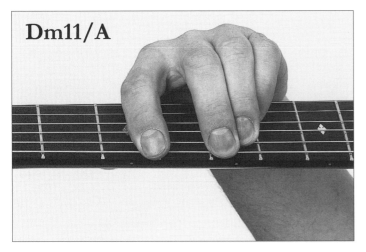

Dm11/A

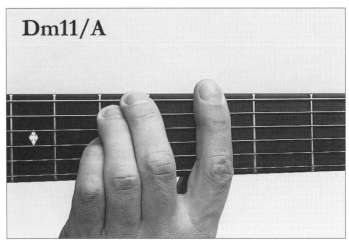

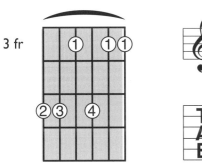

3 fr

```
    3
    3
T   5
A   3
B   5
    5
```

Track 52

'A Hard Day's Night'

One of the most famous – and talked-about – chords in pop history! Guitarists have argued for years over the exact voicing of this chord. It was also originally played on a 12-string, adding to the confusion. However, finger this chord shape, strum, and most people will be able to tell you what song it's from!

E/D

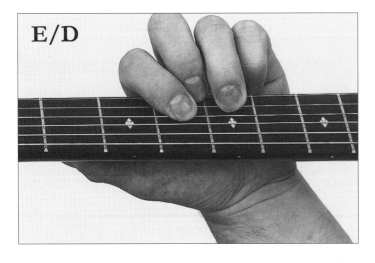

E/D

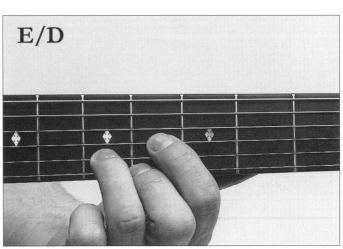

× × ○

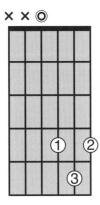

```
    4
    5
T   4
A   0
B
```

Track 53

'Play a D, and move it up a bit'!

This is what you get when you finger a D shape and move it up to the 4th fret. You can try this technique with lots of different chords, all over the fretboard. This particular one was used on Extreme's hit 'Hole Hearted'.

HOW TO DOWNLOAD
YOUR MUSIC TRACKS

1. Carefully remove your Download Card from the inside back cover of this book.

2. On the back of the card is your unique access code. Enter this at www.musicsalesdownloads.com

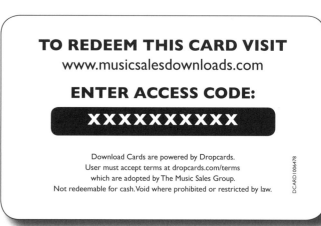

TO REDEEM THIS CARD VISIT
www.musicsalesdownloads.com

ENTER ACCESS CODE:

XXXXXXXXXX

Download Cards are powered by Dropcards.
User must accept terms at dropcards.com/terms
which are adopted by The Music Sales Group.
Not redeemable for cash. Void where prohibited or restricted by law.

DCARD1006478

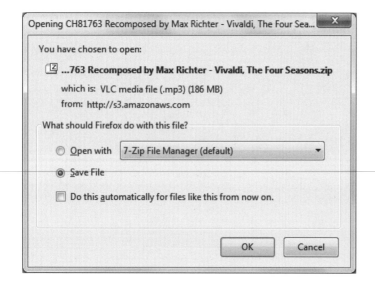

3. Follow the instructions to save your files to your computer*. That's it!

*Appearance of download manager will vary depending upon operating system and web browser.
In case of difficulty when downloading files, please contact dropcards.com/help
Card missing? Please contact music@musicsales.co.uk